THE DALES OF YORK

THE PHOTOGRAPHY OF

HAZEL SANDERSON

CREATIVE MONOCHROME
CONTEMPORARY PORTFOLIO SERIES

HAZEL SANDERSON was born in Romford, Essex and spent most of her formative years in Cambridge. Moving to West Yorkshire in 1968, she at once felt an affinity with the Dales landscape. But it was not until 1982 that her creative aspirations were at last realised through her discovery of the medium of monochrome photography as the means for expressing her sense of wonder and respect for the natural world. Since this time, she has progressed rapidly, gaining her Associateship of the Royal Photographic Society in 1986. A prolific worker, Hazel has staged several exhibitions, undertaken a number of commissions, and has had her work published in several magazines. Although this portfolio concentrates on Hazel's images of her adopted county, her travels throughout the UK and Europe have enabled her to build an impressive and extensive landscape collection.

THE DALES OF YORKSHIRE
The photography of
HAZEL SANDERSON

Published in the UK by Creative Monochrome Ltd,
20 St Peters Road, Croydon, Surrey, CR0 1HD.
© Creative Monochrome Ltd, 1995.

British Library Cataloguing-in-Publication Data:
A catalogue record for this book is available from
the British Library

ISBN 1 873319 17 7
First edition, 1995

Printed in England by Butler & Tanner Ltd,
Caxton Road, Frome, Somerset.

Introduction

Hazel Sanderson

The plaintive calls of a pair of circling curlews over the fell were as primal echoes – unchanged from the days when these valleys were first carved out by glaciers, before their outlines were softened by weathering and river systems to create the beautiful northern uplands as we know them today.

The seasons come and go, with lush meadows in summer and heather-clad moorland above, whilst in winter snows the copious stone walls stand out in sharp relief in linear patterns on the fell sides and in the valleys. The dry-stone walls of millstone-grit and limestone, according to location, greatly influence and characterise this landscape.

The photographs in this portfolio are a celebration of the beauty of this land and of the small things within it. It is a landscape to be treasured and nurtured to ensure its continuity, for it is certain that those who come after us will also need the peace and tranquillity in stressful times which this fair land so readily imparts to those who seek it. Its timelessness is comforting and reassuring in these days when all else can seem transient and insecure.

I first came to the north to live in 1968 when I at once felt an affinity with the landscape and realised that here is where I wanted to be. This feeling has remained and increased over the years as I have looked for and discovered more of the true character of the landscape. There is nothing quite like the exhilaration of being on foot in these wild open spaces; sometimes in their desolate harshness, but also tranformed by wonderful light and cloud shadow into vistas of great beauty. It is within our own nature whether one reacts with feelings of loneliness and apprehension, or excitement and wonder, or simply a sense of peace, but surely no-one can deny the lush pastoral loveliness of the lower valleys.

I have always been intensely aware of the beauty of the natural world and have a strong love and feeling for old buildings and their association with the past and past lives, from the lowliest farmstead to the splendour of abbeys and cathedrals. My desire to record and encapsulate my emotional response to these objects of inspiration was frustrated by my reluctant acceptance of the fact that I had no natural talent for painting or drawing.

In 1982, a friend from girlhood days guided me in the initial stages of photography and I soon came to realise that the camera was the long awaited way to capture and keep what I saw and loved. As time went on, and I became more experienced with printing techniques, my creative need was assuaged and fulfilled.

I then felt the need to have some kind of goal to work towards and so I became a member of the Royal Photographic Society and, in time, submitted a panel of work for the Licienciateship of the Society. Apart from the Leica Postal Portfolio to which I belong, I had no yardstick to measure the quality of my work and so was overjoyed to win through and went on to gain the Associateship in 1986. At the same time, I was offered space at an Ilkley gallery for an exhibition.

In comparison to many photographers, my equipment is very sparse, but then 'little' is often 'good'. I use two Leica R3 single lens reflex bodies and just two lenses – the 60mm macro, which is a wonderful sharp lens for semi-close up work to infinity, and a 90mm. There is much to be said for not having too many lenses to ponder over or to carry about!

There are still those who cannot see the point of black and white photography when there is colour, but that is their loss! The two mediums are so different and both have their own intrinsic beauty and value, but I feel that given the sense of composition and awareness and feeling for light which all photographers must have, black and white gives more scope for creativity. The splendid materials available today give a great choice of film, style of printing and darkroom techniques to be explored and translated to our way of 'seeing', which makes black and white photography so engrossing and satisfying.

Here, in this book of my photographs, I have not attempted to show the whole embracing glories of this northern landscape. Rather, I have selected images which, for me, are the essence distilled from the vastness and variety of the whole. It is often the smaller details which encapsulate the spirit of place as much as the distant horizons. This, then, is my personal homage to the Dales of Yorkshire. I hope that in viewing these images you will be able to share in the great pleasure they have given me.

PORTFOLIO

1
Swaledale, near Thwaite

2
Pennine February – near Tan Hill, Swaledale

3
In Swaledale

4
Bishopdale

5
Swaledale, near Ivelet

6 *(top)* **Nidderdale, near Wath**

7 *(below)* **Arkrigg Common, Wensleydale**

8 *(top)* **Barn at Keld, Swaledale**

9 *(below)* **From Almscliffe Crag, Wharfedale**

10
Woodland at Hackfall, Ripon

11
Beech trees near Thruscross, Washburn Valley

12
Farmstead near Gunnerside, Swaledale

13
Askrigg, Wensleydale

14
Winter at Burnsall, Wharfedale

15
Fountains Abbey, North Yorkshire

16 *(top)* **Angel face, Otley Churchyard**

17 *(below)* **Then and now**

18
'Russ loves Janet', Almscliffe Crag, Wharfedale

19
Window detail, seventeenth century farmhouse, Clifton, Wharfedale

20
Gateway to house at Timble, Wharfedale

21
Gate hasp

22 *(top)* **On the Chevin, Otley**

23 *(below)* **One-time field gate**

24
River driftwood, Wharfe

25
Limb-like ivy clutching the bark

26
Caught!

27
After the rain shower

28
Dry-stone wall and blackberry leaf shadow

29
The fallen leaf

30
Milky way – River Wharfe at The Strid

31

Willow leaves in the quiet current, River Wharfe

32
"The wearing years are many"

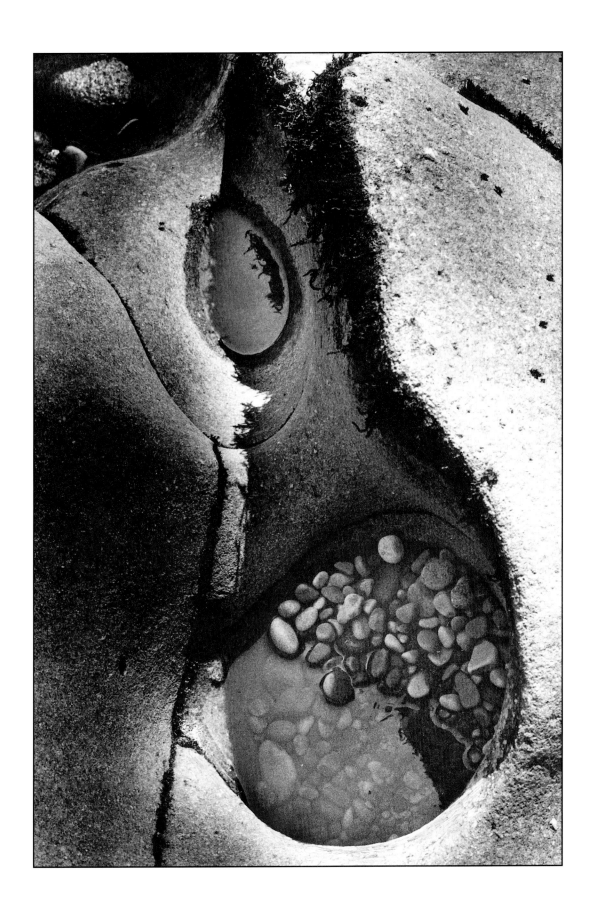

33
Pebble-worn rock, Strid, Wharfedale

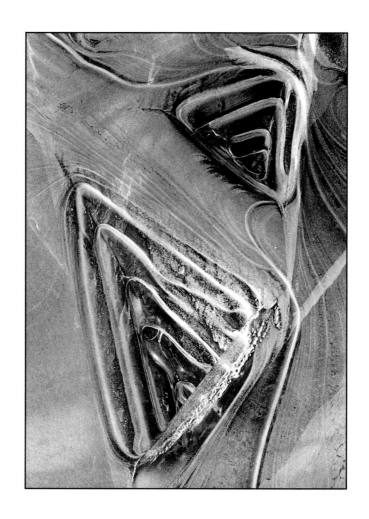

34 *(top)* **Ice triangles**   35 *(below)* **Ice bubbles**

36
Ice wheel

37
Gouthwaite Reservoir, Nidderdale

38
Farmstead at Storiths, Wharfedale

39
Snowscape with sheep

40
The wall

41
Design in winter, Wharfedale

42
Snow fence, Littondale

43
The brook

44
Elm in winter

45 *(top)* **Snow-etched**

46 *(below)* **Hoary hawthorns**

47
Snow tracks and trees

48
Winter at Storiths, Wharfedale

49
Winter sentinel, Wharfedale

PREVIOUS TITLES IN THE
CREATIVE MONOCHROME
CONTEMPORARY PORTFOLIO SERIES

*For further details of the Contemporary Portfolio Series
and a catalogue of Creative Monochrome publications,
please write to Creative Monochrome Limited,
20 St Peters Road, Croydon, Surrey, CR0 1HD, England.*